ISBN 978-1-5281-3569-6
PIBN 10916409

1 MONTH OF
FREE
READING

at

www.ForgottenBooks.com

By purchasing this book you are eligible for one month membership to ForgottenBooks.com, giving you unlimited access to our entire collection of over 1,000,000 titles via our web site and mobile apps.

To claim your free month visit:

www.forgottenbooks.com/free916409

English
Français
Deutsche
Italiano
Español
Português

www.forgottenbooks.com

Mythology Photography **Fiction**
Fishing Christianity **Art** Cooking
Essays Buddhism Freemasonry
Medicine **Biology** Music **Ancient**
Egypt Evolution Carpentry Physics
Dance Geology **Mathematics** Fitness
Shakespeare **Folklore** Yoga Marketing
Confidence Immortality Biographies
Poetry **Psychology** Witchcraft
Electronics Chemistry History **Law**
Accounting **Philosophy** Anthropology
Alchemy Drama Quantum Mechanics
Atheism Sexual Health **Ancient History**
Entrepreneurship Languages Sport
Paleontology Needlework Islam
Metaphysics Investment Archaeology
Parenting Statistics Criminology
Motivational

FEW people know the vast amount of work performed by the Ontario Branch of the Dominion Alliance.

It is steadily at work, holding public meetings, conducting church services, circulating literature, rousing public opinion, perfecting local organization, directing campaigns, promoting law enforcement, and in a thousand and one ways carrying on a great temperance propaganda.

With the many activities of the Alliance this booklet concisely deals. It tells, not of theory only, or what the Alliance "hopes to do," but of actual achievement and definite plans.

The Alliance a Union of the Moral Reform Forces of Ontario.

The Alliance is not a "Temperance Society," indeed, strictly speaking it is not a society at all, but as its name signifies, an "Alliance" of churches and other interested agencies for the purpose of forwarding temperance work.

The Alliance is really the federated church fighting the liquor traffic. It is the agent of the churches in solving the liquor problem, and seeks the highest standard of organized efficiency for the securing of temperance legislation.

The Goal of the Alliance is the Suppression of the Liquor Traffic.

The aim of the Alliance is to create and direct an enlightened public opinion to secure the suppression of the liquor traffic and to unite all churches and moral reform organizations in judicious effort for the attainment of this end.

With nation-wide prohibition in view it works for the enactment and enforcement of all available limitations and restrictions of liquor traffic, assured that this is the shortest road to the ultimate goal.

It also emphasizes the need of electing to all public positions men who are known avowed and trustworthy supporters of its principles and methods.

In its prosecution of this end the Alliance is interdenominational and non-partisan. It deals with one issue only, the suppression of the liquor traffic, and with public men and candidates irrespective of party upon that issue.

The Alliance is a Moral Reform Clearing House and Utilizes Sentiment Created by Various Agencies.

The Alliance unifies the moral reform forces and enables concentration of effort. It is not a rival of any organization, but rather the means by which the work of all is so harmonized and combined that their conjoint efforts will tell more forcefully in the battle for better conditions.

The Alliance does not ask men or women whether they are Conservative or Liberal, Catholic or Protestant; it asks just one simple, straight question, viz., Are you against the liquor traffic and are you willing to co-operate with others of like mind for its destruction? If you do, and are, come on.

It is the clearing house for the effective economical utilization of a temperance sentiment which it is the peculiar province of churches, Sunday schools, young people's societies and temperance organizations to create and strengthen.

An Organization with the People Behind it, and Wisely Guided.

Public confidence in the Alliance, popular interest in its aims, and sympathetic co-operation in its activities, have steadily grown.

The Alliance is doing things.

The representative plan, the large convention, the full discussion, have resulted in ensuring safe, wise, practical demands, and such results as could not have been attained in any other way.

The value of the Alliance efforts has also been great in preventing bad legislation and rousing public opinion to oppose and thwart retrogressive propositions that are made.

The Annual Convention of the Alliance a Provincial Prohibition Parliament.

The Alliance is thoroughly democratic. Each year an Annual Convention is held, to which all churches and sympathetic citizens are entitled to send delegates. At this representative gathering policies and plans are thoroughly discussed and a line of action determined upon.

It is worthy of note, that, for a number of years, every important conclusion reached by the Annual Convention has been by a practically unanimous vote, proving conclusively the soundness and saneness of the Alliance policy and plan.

At the Convention of 1913 over two thousand delegates were in attendance.

The Annual Convention elects officers and an Executive Committee to put into practical effect its decisions.

The Executive Committee appoints a staff of workers, and maintains an office which is headquarters for the temperance work of the Province.

The Alliance in Reality the Official Agent of the Churches of Ontario.

By recent amendments to the Constitution of the Alliance each church denomination within the Province has been given official representation in the Annual Convention.

The presiding officer of, or some other person appointed by, each Presbyterian Synod, Methodist Conference, Provincial Baptist Union, Congregational Union, Anglican Diocese, Roman Catholic Diocese, and of every other Ontario church body having a membership of not less than one thousand within the Province of Ontario, the Chairman and Permanent Secretaries of each organized church department of temperance and moral and social reform, are ex-officio members of the Executive Committee.

The Ontario Alliance Affiliated with Other Provincial Bodies in a Central Dominion Council.

By its Constitution the Ontario Branch of the Dominion Alliance recognizes the Council of the Dominion Alliance as the bond of union between the several provincial branches, and co-operates with it on questions relating to temperance legislation for the Dominion and interprovincial work; and the political platform of the Dominion Alliance, and its declaration of principles is accepted and carried out as far as practicable.

Declaration of Principles of the Council of the Dominion Alliance.

I. That it is neither right nor politic for the State to afford legal protection and sanction to any traffic or system that tends to increase crime, to waste the national resources, to corrupt the social habits and to destroy the health and lives of the people.

II. That the traffic in intoxicating beverages is hostile to the true interests of individuals, and destructive of the order and welfare of society, and ought therefore to be prohibited.

III. That the history and results of all past legislation in regard to the liquor traffic abundantly proves that it is impossible satisfactorily to limit or regulate a system so essentially mischievous in its tendencies.

IV. That no consideration of private gain or public revenue can justify the upholding of a system so utterly wrong in principle, suicidal in policy, and disastrous in results, as the traffic in intoxicating liquors.

V. That the total prohibition of the liquor traffic is in perfect harmony with the principles of justice and liberty, is not restrictive of legitimate commerce, and is essential to the integrity and stability of government, and the welfare of the community.

VI. That, rising above sectarian and party considerations, all citizens should combine to procure an enactment prohibiting the manufacture, importation and sale of intoxicating beverages as affording most efficient aid in removing the appalling evils of intemperance.

Competent Staff Manages the Alliance Business and Publications.

To carry on the enlarging work of the Alliance a competent staff is an absolute necessity. Few organizations have been so fortunate in securing such efficient and self-sacrificing workers as are now engaged under the direction of the Executive Committee of the Alliance.

Giving their whole time to the work in the Province of Ontario are the following men: General Secretary, Rev. Ben. H. Spence; Assistant Secretary, Rev. W. Kettlewell; Office Secretary, D. A. McDermid; Field Secretaries, Rev. R. H. Abraham, D.Sc.; Rev. W. S. MacTavish, D.D.; Rev. Jno. Bailey, M.A.; Rev. John Muir, M.A., and F. W. Duggan.

The Publication Department is in the hands of F. S. Spence as Managing Editor, and N.

F. Caswell, as Associate Editor and Business Manager.

During the summer months' a number of students are employed for campaign work in the sparsely settled districts. These Student Campaign Teams are equipped with a lantern and portable organ, and cover as thoroughly as possible the more remote parts of the Province.

The Alliance Offices Finely Equipped for Efficient Service.

New and more commodious premises for the carrying on of the Alliance business have been secured in a suite of offices at 150 Confederation Life Building, Toronto.

In connection with these new offices there is a public Reading and Writing Room with a temperance reference library and files of temperance papers from all over the world.

Friends of the temperance cause will be made cordially welcome at any time, and information cheerfully furnished in regard to any phase of temperance work.

The growing needs of the expanding work of the Alliance is strikingly illustrated by the increase made necessary in office space, equipment and staff, as shown in the following table:

Year	Sq. Ft. of Office Floor Space	Value of Office Furniture, etc.	Members of staff	Office Assistants	Total Employed
1907	648	$ 350.00	1	3	4
1908	648	524.00	2	5	7
1909	828	693.75	4	7	11
1910	1027	1162.75	5	9	14
1911	1027	1341.05	7	15	22
1912	1400	2434.45	10	18	28
1913	2400	3787.45	11	21	32

N.B.—Many additional helpers are employed during the campaign months of the year.

A Vigorous Educational Propaganda Through Field Day Services, Literature, Etc.

Recognizing that legislation to be permanent and effective must be based upon the intelligent convictions of the electorate, the Alliance seeks to develop such a body of educated public opinion against the liquor traffic in the Province of Ontario as will support an aggressive, progressive, temperance policy.

Alliance Representatives Manned Nearly Three Thousand Pulpits in Field Day Services Last Year.

The fact that the various Churches, through their highest courts, have condemned the barroom, and are allying themselves for its extinction, is strikingly emphasized by the ''Alliance Field Day.'' This actual bringing of the Churches into closer touch with one another, by and through the Alliance, is of incalculable educational and inspirational value in the fight for better social conditions.

In the year 1912 the following services were held: Anglican, 188; Baptist, 257; Congregational, 37; Methodist, 1,105; Presbyterian, 729; Miscellaneous and Union services, 162. A total of 2,473.

During the present year this work has increased and with the tremendous campaign now in progress, and the greater interest in connection with the temperance reform, it is expected that Field Day work will be still further enlarged and strengthened.

Thorough Organization of Every County, City, Town, Village and Township the Alliance Ideal.

In affiliation with the Provincial Alliance, County Alliances have been formed in nearly every County in the Province, and substantial progress has been made in organizing the municipalities within each County along uniform lines.

Our ideal is a working union of the temperance electors in every polling sub-division in the Province, united in municipal organizations by townships, towns, villages and cities; these again co-related and co-operating in a County Alliance; the County Alliances bound together in our provincial organization. Thus we will have organized and ready for any emergency a great fighting organization.

For the purpose of strengthening and facilitating the work of organization, the Province has been divided into six districts, with a Field Secretary in charge of each, who keeps in close touch with every detail of the work.

Legislation, Local and Provincial, the Natural Result of Educational Work.

Local Option is the main legislative method being used at present in the Province. This enables the local municipalities to rid themselves of their share of the burden of the bar.

Where Local Option is not immediately attainable we try to further restrict the traffic by license reduction.

In New Ontario campaigns are being carried on to procure the enactment of the Canada Temperance Act.

Continuous effort is made to secure such amendments to the Liquor License Act as will be helpful to our cause.

Whatever method will crystalize the sentiment of the community into effective legislation, locally or provincially, the Alliance will consistently and persistently work for.

Inspiring Record of Success in Many Local Option Contests.

The following table shows the number of Local Option contests, and the result of the voting, also the total number of licenses granted for the years 1906-1913:

Year	No. of Con-tests	Carried L. O.	Held up by 3-5	Maj Ag. L. O.	Licenses
1906	70	59	..	11	2521
1907	100	44	41	15	2432
1908	84	31	29	24	2328
1909	56	21	22	13	2200
1910	158	77	55	26	1938
1911	81	26	30	25	1836
1912	69	18	21	30	1740
1913	77	26	37	14	1620
Total	695	302	235	158	

In January, 1914, Local Option By-laws will be submitted in 40 or 50 municipalities.

Three-fifths of the Ontario Municipalities are Now Under Prohibition.

In 1906 there were 310 more municipalities under license than under prohibition, in 1913 there are 169 more under prohibition than under license.

The following diagram shows the total number of municipalities with the number under license and under prohibition in the Province for the years 1906-1913:

Year	Total Munici-palities	Wet	Dry	Maj. Wet	Maj. Dry
1906	794	552	242	310	...
1907	794	508	286	222	...
1908	804	492	312	180	...
1909	807	475	332	143	...
1910	812	407	405	2	...
1911	822	380	440	...	60
1912	828	365	463	...	98
1913	835	333	502	...	169

Majority of Ontario Citizens Have Declared for Prohibition—One, Million Now Live in Dry Territory.

In the last ten years the aggregate vote "for" and "against" Local Option in 725 contests shows the enormous majority of 56,863 for the abolition of the entire retail sale of intoxicating liquor.

1,090,502 of Ontario's population live in communities which have outlawed the liquor traffic.

1,432,772 live in communities in which licenses are granted, but of these 311,460 are in municipalities where a majority has been polled in favor of Local Option. Thus the sentiment of the people as expressed in our Local Option campaigns and in other ways shows 1,401,962 in favor of local prohibition; 1,121,312 that have not yet declared against license.

It will thus be seen that the sentiment of the Province of Ontario is overwhelmingly against the liquor traffic.

When Local Option By-laws are Passed They Stay Passed.

Proof of the success of Local Option is the satisfaction with its operation, as shown in the history of attempts to repeal the measure.

The following table gives the result of repeal voting for the past three years:

	1911	1912	1913	Ttl.
Possible contests	134	178	240	552
No vote	131	163	218	522
Local Op. sustained..	3	15	21	39
Local Op. repealed...	..	..	1	1

Every effort is being made to maintain this magnificent record.

Law Enforcement the Key to Permanence.

Increasing attention is being given to the work of law enforcement. A special law enforcement file is kept, the object being to maintain regular correspondence with all parts of the Province and to give advice and assistance wherever possible, particular attention being given to the work of seeing that appointed officers perform their duty.

The Extension of Local Option is Making Provincial Action Increasingly Necessary.

As Local Option territory increases the sphere of operation by the Local Option method decreases and the necessity is more clearly seen for Province-wide legislation, thus the Local Option method is forcing the issue along provincial lines.

This again compels the Alliance to more actively participate in electoral work, and it is doing so in an absolutely non-partisan way.

The Pioneer a Power for Good in the Province.

The circulation of the Pioneer, the weekly paper published by the Alliance, has increased till now nearly twenty-three thousand copies go each week into twenty-three thousand homes in the Province of Ontario, carrying information and giving inspiration to our workers everywhere.

The growth of the Pioneer is shown by the following table which gives the number of names upon the mailing list on the first of January of each year:

On January 1st, 1906	4,811
" " " 1907	5,194
" " " 1908	5,655
" " 1909	7,890
" 1910	9,750
1911	13,672
1912	19,904
" " " 1913	21,725
On October 1st, 1913	22,592

Munitions of War Supplied by Publication Department.

All the necessary forms of petition and by-laws for Local Option and Canada Temperance Act campaigns, instructions for agents at the polls, etc., are supplied gratuitously wherever needed throughout the Province.

Books, pamphlets, leaflets, posters, cards, blotters, buttons, badges and other campaign literature are also issued from time to time as necessary.

Lantern slides and illustrative charts are also available for workers and speakers throughout the Province.

The Financial Management of the Alliance Carefully Controlled by Capable Committee.

The utmost care is exercised regarding the financial management of the Alliance. All accounts are examined and passed by a competent committee and payment is made by cheque signed by the Treasurer and countersigned by the Chairman of the Finance Committee.

The Alliance books and accounts are carefully audited each year by a firm of chartered accountants, and a detailed statement submitted to the Annual Convention.

The Alliance officers feel that all contributions are received in trust for the furtherance of the temperance cause, and the most rigid economy and careful management is exercised in their disbursement.

Splendid Results Secured with Moderate Expenditure.

All the Alliance forces are maintained, expenses paid, literature printed and distributed, organization effected, campaigns carried on, meetings and services held and victories gained on an income less than that of the average bar-room in the City of Toronto.

There are single churches in the Province which raise more money than the Alliance receives from all sources for its temperance work.

The work of the Alliance is essentially team work. It is a co-operative agency. Its support does not come mainly from the large gifts of the select few, but from the modest contributions of the many.

The destruction of the liquor traffic would mean the promotion of civic righteousness and economic development. No better investment of money or effort can possibly be made along reform lines than in this work of "Nation Building."

The Conflict is Well Defined—it is Between the "Alliance" and the "Trade."

The Alliance does not claim to be the only agency fighting the liquor traffic. It gladly recognizes the fundamental work done by the churches and the many auxiliary agencies, scientific and otherwise, that are creating public opinion, but it is only by the combination of these forces and the crystallization of sentiment into legislation, that the organized forces of the liquor traffic can be met and destroyed.

The traffic is essentially selfish, arrogant, mercenary, and unscrupulous. Its allies are the corrupt and vicious elements of society, which batten upon the saloon; the politician who truckles or is venal; the short-sighted business man who has not the courage to do right; the lazy or indifferent "good" ('good' for nothing) man who shirks his duty.

Right is winning. The traffic is doomed. A modern Christian civilization is outgrowing this great evil.

"For life shall on and upward go.
The eternal step of progress beats
To that great anthem, calm and slow,
Which God repeats."

Bouquets from Opponents.

From the "*Wine and Spirit Journal,*" the official organ of the licensed trade of the Province of Ontario, the following extracts are taken:

"The teetotal party in Ontario is girding up its loins, stiffening its backbone, and sharpening its weapons for a prodigious assault upon the wine and spirit trade next January.

There is no disguising the fact that the trade is now facing a very critical period of its existence. The teetotal party is preparing to make a supreme effort. . . . .

Owing to its affiliation with church bodies the Alliance has command of a very large sum, and to offset this it is absolutely necessary that the licensed trade generally throughout the province should rally to the defence of those of its members whose interests are threatened. . . . .

The teetotal party is thoroughly organized. There is not a member of the licensed trade, from the smallest roadside tavern to the biggest hotel in the biggest city of the province, whose interests are not menaced. . . . .

It is only through a united body such as the Licensed Trade Association that the hotelkeeper and shopkeeper in this province can hope to fight the Dominion Alliance. . . . .

The Alliance makes the most of church influence . . . and its outlay on speakers, literature and canvassing is prodigious. To combat this effectually, and to scotch at any rate, if not to kill, the efforts of its opponents, the "Trade" must stand solidly together."

The wholesome fear entertained for the Alliance in certain quarters is a strong testimony to its effective work.

REMEMBER
THE ALLIANCE IN YOUR WILL

FORM OF BEQUEST.

I give and bequeath to the Ontario Branch of the Dominion Alliance the sum of...Dollars, to be used and applied for the purpose of Temperance work in the Province of Ontario.